All Hail Nikey Pasco-Dunston

"Giving anything but a 5 star would be ridiculous. I am not usually a fan of poetry, but I thought I would try it all. This is the kind of poetry that makes you wonder what it would have been like during the Harlem Renaissance to be there with Langston Hughes. It was so deep, but understandable. So emotional, and so seductive. An amazing addition to my collection of authors to be on the look-out for."

- Tabitha Sharpe, author of Unhinged, on Writings On My Wall, Amazon Kindle Edition.

"This book is phenomenal, every poem that she wrote in here, had a clear and thought provoking message inside that you can understand and learn from. This is a must read, Writings On My Wall is very inspirational."

- Carlos Torres, author and director of Game of Redemption, on Writings On My Wall, Amazon Kindle Edition.

"This book should be required reading to young women around the world in high school. I believe that you share very valuable information that helps women to learn how to protect their mental and physical well-being."

- Karolyn Huddleston, author of Master of Deception, on Scars.

"The book actually brought back a few memories of my past. To read detail after detail and to know the author is here NOW writing about it... Nobody BUT GOD!! I think this book should be available to all girl group homes! To let them know, that they're not alone and YES they STILL have a chance!! GREAT BOOK NIKEY... continue to tell your story!!!"

- N. Dorris, author of Dirty Little Secrets, on Scars.

Writings On MY WALL

Lyrical Thoughts Of A Queen

Contents

Dedication

I want to dedicate this poetic collection to my great-grandparents, Robert & Moselle Bohannon. Nana and Grandpa you two helped raise me and encouraged me to read and write poetry before I entered Kindergarten... and I thank you for that from the pit of my heart. I wish I could have said these words to you both before y'all passed away. Although you both are no longer flesh on earth your energy lives on and within me.

It's alright to do three dedication's right? Well this is my book so I will. I also want to dedicate this poetic collection to the amazing King that I married – Eddie Dunston II. I interrupt you during football and basketball games and even when you're creating beats just so you can hear my poems and you never complain. You have been so supportive since day one and that's why I will always be your rider baby!

Lastly, I must dedicate this poetic collection to my beautiful Mummie. Goddess you too have always encouraged me to write poetry, songs, and draw as far back as I can remember. You framed my poetry with the matching artwork that I drew and you cheered me on when I wanted to be the next big rapper/singer. No matter what we've been through – the positive things you've done will always outweigh any negative memory. I truly appreciate everything you've done for me... I love all of y'all to the universe and back!

The Art of Love Making

THE ART OF LOVE MAKING

Let's exchange vibes and see where it leads

Let's speak on our essence as we build positive frequencies

There's nothing greater than joining our masculine and feminine energies

Expanding our consciousness with pure spiritual practice

As I undress you and you undress me

I feel at peace and I love it.

When our minds are on the same level I am wide open

Focusing on our breath and touch - meditation

As we massage each other bodies to full relaxation

Raising our awareness with genital stimulation

We yearn for each other more, yet we are patient

I feel at peace and I love it.

I know your desires and I am here to submit

Explore my body with your mouth and I will explore yours

Indulge sweetly in this divine kiss

Give yourself completely to me and I'll give myself completely to you

I feel at peace and I love it.

Carnal knowledge is power and I luxuriate in every bit

I appreciate every inch that you give me

The best thing I did was let you in me

Inside of my mind, my soul has been rejuvenated

I feel at peace and I love it.

This long wait has been oh-so worth waiting

I never knew a love so genuine than yours

Every time our bodies touch I fall deeper in love

It's an extraordinary adoration

I am more than grateful for every single experience

I'm in so much peace and I love it.

STIMULATION

The lighting is dim
Thirty-three candles are lit
With a relaxing aromatherapy scent
I am inviting you in.

Jet black silk sheets,
Drape loose on my California King
Champagne sheer and lace lingerie
Hugging my enticing physique.

With a peek-a-boo thong,
I will give you a sneak peek
As I wine in front of you
Slow and seductively.

As the passion burns,
My mind constantly yearns
You are all that I want
I am craving for you.

All I need is your touch
The thought gives me a sensation
A feeling I've been needing so much
Light my fire.

With every spark and flame,
My body calls your name

You are the one that I desire
Take me higher.

Somewhere on cloud nine,
I felt your tongue go down my spine
I felt your fingers caress my inner thighs
As I close my eyes.

I gently fondle my gem,
Then I open up to let you in
Your mouth is so amazing
You took me there.

And I don't want to leave,
I am in love with this climax
The experience of external ecstasy
This feeling is rare.

Please, take your time,
Don't rush this kind of greatness
This is something exclusive
A humid love story in the making.

My back is slightly arched
My legs are uncontrollably shaking
My sheets are wet from the stimulation
The power of imagination.

It's no secret how much I want you,
But the question is, do you want me to?

DO YOU MIND

Do you mind if I whisper something sultry into your mind?

The succulence of my word play

Will make your thoughts race

Into another time - dimension

Just listen…

It is tantalizing.

It is pleasing.

It is mesmerizing.

It is intriguing.

It is your biggest fantasy to the sixth power

Your inclination I will empower

Your temple I will shower.

Just visualize you

Connecting with me

Visualize our waves

Our forcible frequencies

Our irresistible vibes

You cannot deny - what is meant to be

These sensual things that only you can see

These sensual things that happen between you and me

As they go deeper and deeper

So deep inside of your dreams

Your visual is bright and I can make it clearer.

Invite me into your sensuous vision...

Do you mind if I come in?

Let's exchange thoughts and see what happens

Manifesting the perceptibility, as you feel me caressing your skin -

Gently.

Soft touches to your intellect

Ya feel me?

Easing my way slowly past your chest

Easing my way, I'm yearning for your head

I chose you because you are the best

I chose you because I am diggin' your head - brain

We know that everyone wants it.

I pity the bone that lacks this type of competence

Your consciousness...

Your knowledge.

Your cognition entices me on a whole different level

I understand that it's our minds that are so
equally parallel

I'm deeply in love because you're so intellectual

Your wisdom is so effectual

You make my temperature rise

Oh my...Sapiosexual.

Do you mind if I come inside?

ECSTASY

In the dawn you rise high,
Like the sun gleaming in the sky

Glistening and shining,
As hard as a black diamond

Your diamond is most wanted;
Your rays are so potent

Inside of me,
I'm experiencing divine ecstasy.

In my eyes,
You are all that I see

In my mind,
You are all that I need

That magic potion,
Doubling up on that Vitamin D

Inside of me,
I'm experiencing divine ecstasy.

When our minds connect,
Power rises between our intellect

Pay attention,
We are yoked to the rhythm

Your supreme seeds,
Cultivated deeply within me

Inside of me,
I'm experiencing divine ecstasy.

TAKE YOUR TIME

I've been waiting all day to have you in my presence

Just to feel your smooth skin on top of mine

Imagining your body in between my thighs

The thought of your tongue has been on my mind

Slowly slipping off my black Carine Gilson

Fully lined in silk satin

Sexy and shimmering in my Lurex Collection

As my robe comes down

Your strength comes up

You gently lick around my breasts

And tease my nipples with your tongue

As your masculine hands caress my soft round butt

I am loving every moment

My heart is racing and I cannot control it

It is about to happen

As I lay down with my legs spread wide open

Take your time baby I'm focused

We don't have to rush this

I am panting heavily

This feeling has taken over me

I feel the moisture every time I slip inside

I feel the moisture every time I close my eyes

The pleasure is all mine.

For The Love of Foreplay

I am slowly making my way up your beautiful body

Caressing your feet and running my tongue across your skin

Slowly approaching your mid-section

You're aroused

Turned on

Leaking like a faucet

I play with it for a little and then I gently kiss it

Continuing my path all the way up

I look you in your eyes and you grab on my butt

Damn it feels so good...

Kissing your chest and licking on your nipples

You are rubbing my breasts as I kiss on your neck

Our eyes connect as our lips finally meet

Heavy breathing and caressing

The feeling is one of a kind

Climaxing as we stare in each other's eyes

I never knew that foreplay could be this sweet.

Thoughts

Whispers and thoughts…

Let me give your body what it wants.

Treat your body like the temple it is…

Delivering what it has been yearning for.

I will keep it low as I ride your mind slow and with ease…

Your whole mental and physical I will please.

I'm just that nice…

Climaxation

No masturbating

No penetrating

Yet your toes are curling and your body is sweating…

I got your mind going wild.

Enjoy this ride because the pleasure is all mine.

This feeling takes time…

Sit back, relax, close your eyes and release.

Can you handle a goddess like me?

Limitless Love

LOVE

Love

Love

I never knew love

No, I never knew love like this

The power of your touch

Completely fills me up

Thought I could never ever love

Creating your potion

The feeling got me floating

It has my mind roaming in love

Love

Love

I never knew love

No, I never knew love like this

The way you pull and stroke it

Has me completely focused

I'm soaked, drowning

Overdosing from love

Love

Love

I never knew love

No, I never knew love like this.

YOU

I am his moon and he is my sun,

As we lie here in complete tranquility

Drenching in divine love.

You are so perfect,

So perfectly sun-kissed.

I see no wrong in you,

You are the definition of amazing.

You bring out the best of me,

A beautiful creation.

You are...

The fire in my eyes,

The blood in my heart,

The air that I breathe,

Spiritually you uplift me.

You never put me down,

As you tap into my mind subconsciously.

You are all that I need.

MY ALL

Looking back on when we first met
I never thought that we would be
You became my lover and friend
You became my everything.
No storm too powerful
No argument worth letting us go
You've given your heart to me
You became my everything.
When I needed you most
You remained at my side
Loyal to the grain
You are always true
You became my everything.
No matter what anyone says
There is no tearing us apart
My pride
My joy
My everything

My all.

SPECIAL YOU ARE

There is no choice
No competition
You are the full package
It's a win-win
Therefore, you've won
From the moment I saw you
I knew that you were
The one.

Your sexy eyes and full flips
Your brown skin and smooth kiss
I indulge in full bliss
Our romance is on ten
Your love is everlasting
No one could ever replace you
You are unique in so many ways
That is why my heart chose you

So special you are...a dream come true.

EVERYTHING

I never thought we would be like this

In love not giving a damn what no one thinks

When I do for you

You do for me

Vice versa like it's supposed to be

We've been facing the world without a bit of fear

I'll fight the next one because our love is rear

When my heart is in pain

So hurt you'll wipe my tears

You're the only Negus real

The only one I feel

If another tried to scoop me

I promise you he'll know the deal

We're sealed tight like a legal bond

If they try to wild-out, you know I'll be your Bon

Smith and Wesson at my side you know I'll set it off

I gave my all for you

You gave your all to me

Shining bright

Black diamond

I ain't giving you up

You're my everything.

9ᵀᴴ WONDER

I never knew how to love sincerely...

Until I was blessed with an angelic being that grew inside of me.

The greatest creations on earth come from the most-high

And that I cannot deny.

It is clear to me...

Yes, I understand.

I breathe

I see

I cry

I feel

I love so deep

I am aware that it is within me.

To nurture and heal...

I created life and that is the greatest emotion that one could ever feel.

LOVE WITH YOU

The amount of love that I have for you is beyond words spoken

I am glad that stars aligned us

I am joyous to be chosen

Your love is so golden

Your touch makes me open

Your sensual voice sends chill's up my spine

The way you make love to me brings tears to my eyes

Caressing my body as you access my temple slowly

I can't control it...

I'm falling deeper and deeper.

Secrets

What we have is beyond deep

We have stepped into the oceans that only we can feel and see

Our waters meet smoothly coming together so beautifully

Intellectually you satisfy my needs

But only we can see this magic

Only we can feel this chemistry

It is us that knows this passion

The indecent risks that we are taking

For the sake of our pleasure

Passionate love making

You allowed me in and now you're addicted

This divine sin had me conflicted

Now I am the least bit confused

I know what I want and it is you

I know what I need and it is still you

I have never met someone quite like you before

Our lives are different but somehow we met and explored each other's minds

If you ever need me, I will be at your side

Without question, I am here

I am your protection

Your strength

Your motivation

Your slayer

Destroying any competition

Because I - refuse - to lose - you

My sun

You give me light

And my light brightens your darkest nights

Just talk to me...

I am listening

It was never supposed to be like this...

Something so innocent turned into our flaming secret...

The desire burns within my soul...

You've filled that void

No more hole

I will love you eternally

Until our next lifetime, our bodies will meet...again

I will forever and always love you

My secret lover

My friend.

The Connection

Subtle whispers
I can hear your thoughts miles away
Your mind is racing...

I wonder what she's thinking?
Does she think I'm attractive?
Am I even her type?
The things I would do to her if I had just one night.

You can see my face
You can feel my body
Your mouth is all over me
How do I taste?

If I could simply please her
Take my time and give her what she deserves
She's so seductive
I wonder if she wants me?

I want you more than you think
I fall asleep with you on my mind
You are steady in my dreams...

She's in my dreams as I explore her deepest fantasies
I know she's a freak behind closed doors
I'll have her yearning for more.

I can feel your thoughts tingling through my body
The more I fiend for you
The more you want me...

Since I first laid eyes on her
My thoughts were lost as I craved for her touch
I can't take this feeling any longer
It is me who she wants...

At last, our bodies softly meet
You are everything that I envisioned you to be
Loving you is so amazing.

Made For A King

Natural curves that flow like waves

That good hair because I'm African made

It was done purposely and I am not the least bit sorry

No, I am not sorry

Nor am I ashamed

For what reason?

It was done out of love because what is meant to be will be

Born to be the most emulated being on the face earth

The essence of my existence was established since the goddess gave birth to an Empress

A bona fide Queen

With alluring lips and hips

With intellect and strength to move mountains

That is because I am the lioness

Fearless to cross perilous rivers

My words pump fear through vessels straight to the heart

Nonstop power

I have nonstop influence

My desire is to be greater than what is expected

I am top of the line selected

Detailed and carefully put together when I was created

Be careful because I am gentle

I may be strong but I am also feeble

My entire being was made for my equal

My coordinate is brown with full lips and kinky hair

The kind of hair that many call naps

But I call it that ether

Yeah...

I love that ether 9 hair

The beauty of his coils are so breathtaking I swear

I am in love with his gray matter and the melanin in his eyes

I know the feeling is mutual because he too is in love with mine

I was made for only a King

And with a King, I will live my life.

Enchanted Thoughts

Loving everything about you

My mind, body, and soul somehow connect with yours

For years I prayed

Then I began to patiently wait for your arrival

It is to the point that I don't want to let you go

Holding on to your invisible hand with all my might

Physically sleeping alone yet I'm with you at night

There is magic in this association

But the distance is not right

Scared that you may forget my love for you

It is so genuine and pure

Rich like honey and fresh like the morning dew

I yearn for you

Longing to be at your side

I thought I had no more feelings left

This love came by surprise yet I am not surprised

We were destined to meet

Destined to touch souls and bond eternally

I am yours.

Overload

The thought of your strong arms holding me close does the most - to me...

I am loving your affection and the way that you rub on me

Your smile

Your energy

I am loving the attention that you are giving to me

It is beyond what I have ever imagined

I am beyond at ease

This feeling is doing something magical to me

It has taken me on a natural high of security

I can breathe...again

Inhale and exhaling these vigorous frequencies

Flowing through my body

Touching every millimeter of me

Down to the tip of my toes

I am on overload

'Bout ready to explode

Letting these emotions grow to another level

And I ain't trying to let go

You are giving me everything that I need.

Affliction

SERPENT

Lacerations to my mental

So rooted

Contoured in sorrow

The affliction had taken over

With no hope for tomorrow

Constant burns in scrapes

Please take this pain away

I've been living in shame

In hopes that these feelings will fade

No matter what direction I prayed

Nothing seemed to change

I gave my life to you

I prayed and prayed to you

Dear God, what did I do?

To deserve this kind of agony

Extending so deep inside me

My mind

My soul

My body

The wounds are deep past the layers of my skin

I'm so broken up that I let you in

I let you in and now I'm broken

I could have avoided any and all disappointments

I blindly welcomed the beast in

Gradually injecting its venom

Slowly carrying out its magic

The figure will have you deluded

It comes in all shapes, shades, and sizes

The future had me blinded

Not focused on the present

Throughout all of the praying

I learned a crucial lesson

Never trust a serpent –

just keep your distance.

BLESSING IN DISGUISE

With open arms and so much love
I gave you my trust
I gave you the keys to my whip
I opened up and gave you the keys to my crib
I never thought for one second that you would betray me
But you did...
Yes, you did.

You took my kindness for granted
You took my heart and used it
You took my body and abused it
You stole my heart and viciously tore it apart
And I stood there dying internally.

You are a thief –
And I don't fuck with thieves.
Because they have the capability of murder.
But before you murder me

I will annihilate you.

I will exterminate the pain
I will eradicate the trauma that you caused to my brain
Have you no shame?
Of course not...
But these feelings will fade.

I've come to realize,
That you were my blessing in disguise.
You broke my heart but you healed my eyes
They say "love is blind" and they are right
You broke my trust
But you've given me sight
You destroyed my confidence
But I will be alright.

You battered my heart severely
And you've taken so much from me
But you have given more
Strength
Vision

The courage to endure...

Pain at an ultimate high

Resilience that goes further than the sky.

There is no limit

You've given me the kind of strength that is endless

The courage to face my fears

The affirmation to finally release my tears...

The power of love.

FALLING

I'm falling

The wind blows like a sharp whistle
Wrapping my frame
I can hardly breathe
The feeling is not the same
Life was once so warm and gentle

The sol's beams are cold
Chipping away at my heart
I can't believe this happened
Everything has come to a halt
The pieces cannot fit these holes
I can't catch myself

I'm falling.

BROKEN

When trust becomes just a word that is commonly used

You will second guess everything

Due to it being passed around and abused

Nothing makes sense

I can no longer put my trust into you

You once had the best of me

Anything you wanted was yours

But now you destroyed that part of me

Are you happy that you broke me?

Are you satisfied that you destroyed me?

You have created a savage

I am convinced that I may never fully heal

It felt like a tsunami hit my lungs

Now I am struggling to breathe

I'm drowning

These ungodly feelings you can have it

I am giving them back to you

Take it!

You entered my life when I was whole

My energy was high

There was nothing but pleasant vibes through my soul

I'm so nauseous from this madness

My heart has been shattered.

DISLOYALTY

The bond was so tight

So tight that air could not slip through

There was nothing or no one that could break it

The thought was unimaginable

It was heavily frowned upon

The idea was forsaken

So when I told you my deepest secrets

That was because I believed in you

I was convinced that you would keep them

Stored in your memory

Locked away but still lingering in your mind

You knew what would bruise me

You knew what would make me cry

You knew what would tear me down inside

Yet you did not care about me

Don't mistake my tears for sadness

Don't misconstrue my sorrow as weakness

It is deeper than your eyes can see

Tears of anger from your betrayal

I allowed you to burn me numerous times

And that puts the shame on me

These tears fall due to my own stubbornness

They fall from my own disloyalty.

NO ONE

When no one else was there,
I was right at your side.
Loving you...

When no one else spared their ear,
I quickly loaned you mine.
Hearing you...

When no one else gave you a dime,
I gave you all of my time.
Deserving you...

When there was no one else,
There was always me.
Here for you...

No matter what,

I am here.

No matter how far,

I was there.

You took my kindness for weakness...

You took my availability for granted...

Because I was concerned and no one else was.

No one,

No, no one.

There was no one but me.

THE REALIZATION

As much as I cry,

No one sees my tears...

As much as I am scared of pain,

No one sees my fears.

As much as I want to leave,

No one is holding me here.

I stay because loneliness is a thing that I fear.

I stay because "no one else will want me" is the thing that I hear...

And I believe it...

I am washed up

I am unwanted.

As much as I struggle,

No one knows of my troubles...

Not a soul knows about my struggle.

As much as I yearn for your acceptance...
I am more than grateful for each lesson.
I thank the stars above for my every blessing...
That you gave to me
It is those same very stars that I put my faith in.

As much as I want to breakdown...
I know I should not throw my towel to the ground.
I keep on, quietly, without a sound.

As much as I scream and cry in the inside,
I seriously want to release this agony out loud.
But my mind won't let me...
I don't want to be looked at differently.
I don't want to be judged...
As much as I held back saying this
all I need is your love.

I am desperate for your attention...
I am in need of your time and affection.
I am tired of the heartache
Scars open from depression.

Non-stop praying for a new beginning

How much longer do I have to keep praying?

As much as I want this to work

I have grown to realize my worth

And you are no longer worth my time.

MOVING ON

Sometimes you wonder why they say everything happens for a reason?

Those times that you ask yourself

"Why am I still breathing?"

So much lies and betrayal

You never know who to trust

I give my all to you

I know you won't ever slip up

I lay down in pain

I close my eyes to pray...

"Give me strength and the power to accept and move on"

My prayer gets deeper

As my body gets weaker

Raised to be independent and strong

Told to use my brain....

You have to be real smart.

Yeah, that's the song that I sang

Every day at the park

The more I grow...the more I see.

Be independent because you really don't have me.

Be strong because you'll have to fight off the horrible memories.

Be smart because you'll need to know how to survive in the streets.

Smart I am...

Independent...

Yeah, that too.

Strength is what I'm missing

And it is all because of you!

I'm done with the fake smiles.

I'm done with pretending I'm not hurt.

I'm done with pretending like I don't care.

Life is too short and I don't have 9 lives to spare.

I am moving on.

The Dilemma

Why must you get so loud?

There is no need to shout about since I am standing so near

My ears are far from deaf

I can hear you

I hear you loud and clear

Let us speak like mature individuals

So our points can be understood

I don't care to express myself in such an ugly manner

Yelling and arguing is not my kind of thing

Fussing and fighting does nothing for me

When I ask a question

You feel like you're under cross-examination

When I make a statement

You feel like I am offending you

No matter what I say

There seems to be an issue

An argument

I do not mean to go against you

Or be such a problem

I come off with a mellow tone

And you still feel threatened

Something is not right

There is something that I am missing

I never wanted it to be this way

There are only two options left

Do I leave or do I stay?

And you will not make that decision.

Malaise

I dry my eyes as I shed tears of sorrow

Not a soul knows my pain

My head stays high and I smile

With a positive state of mind

I know this feeling will not last forever

Maybe tomorrow or the next day

But not forever

This is not what life is about

Please take this feeling away

Give me a great reason to stay.

The Rebirth

Heartache pounding like drums

Stabbing sharp like a butcher knife

Slit throat

I'm holding my neck gripping it tight

I feel like I am about to die

Curled up like a fetus

Why did you have to do this to me?

You took away my Life

You took away my everything

And now I am here dying in agony

This is not how I wanted life to be

But this is the life that I choose to leave

With you, I've been so disconnected from reality

With you, I've been so disconnected from my family

But not anymore

I am leaving this life

I am leaving this continuous misery

My breath is almost gone

You successfully drained away my energy

My heart is slowly stopping

You have not won because this is my new beginning

The old me is dead and I'm back with a new life

This is the rebirth

Blood flowing through my veins

I have been reborn.

Access Denied

You hurt me

You betrayed me

You took my love for granted

Granted that you take my kindness for weakness

Then you look me in my eyes and to utter nonsense lies

Your famous lie of all time is, "I'm sorry."

Constant apologies

"Oh baby please"

The stupidity never ends

And I'm supposed to accept it?

No, it's rejected.

Damaged Chronicles

All this time I devoted to you

Lost in time believing the lies

My mind was focused on you

So focused I didn't hear my own cries

Hoping, praying and talking to whoever is in the air listening

I only wanted what was best but you started tripping

My heart was beating for you

But you did not care about my feelings

All of the emotions that overcame me

I felt myself slipping

My mind was going crazy

The first time I let you slide

Is when I let my soul die

I didn't flip out or question your absence

I needed no reason why

I sat back and kept quiet like I thought I should

The second time around, you did not answer my calls

Your excuse was that you didn't hear the phone ring at all

I knew then that it was bull but I held on to the loose screws

In hopes that they would tighten

To myself, I was steady lying

I could not handle the ugly truth

Looking for love in all the wrong places

Not giving a damn about who I was dating or screwing

I was looking for security and I thought that I found it within you and

My heart was missing love...

So empty due to lack of affection and abandonment

But then I let my guards down and gave you my world

I trusted you with every inch of my being

I knew what you were doing but I could not face it and

I was in absolute disbelief that you were creeping

The lying, scheming, and cheating

Smiling in my face knowing that you were disloyal to me and

You're so double sided

Lord knows that I could not take it

So I did what I knew to do best

I released that inner darkness

The beast that I fight to suppress

That beast I kept hidden away

So far away but it slowly crept out

I tried to hold it back

But you deliberately destroyed me mentally

Now the villain in my head wants to play with you.

The Inundation

Since the inner darkness revealed itself nothing has been the same

I can see through the shadows in this cold, cold world

You want me to forget what you did but the pain severely aches

The process of termination is not as easy as you think

There is a trigger being constantly squeezed like an automatic Ruger

Releasing bullets of murderous memories

When will it be over?

When will this end?

Give me my life back

I am slowly drowning.

Most Wanted

PRAISE YE

There is no you without there being a me
Just like there are no stars without the galaxy.

There is no you without there being a me
Just like there is no fruit without there being a seed.
Planted within me...

There is no you without there being a me
Goddess of all...
A mother
A Queen.

There is no you without there being a me
And all I ask from you is to respect the queen.

SHE IS A QUEEN

She is so deep like your roots
Everything she says is the truth
She speaks and uplifts our youth
Looking lovely in her desired melanin
As she proudly stands up for our men
Whenever she talks they hush and they listen.

We appreciate every bit of her compassion
It is her on-going dedication that keeps our attention
Her passion for education is what instills her with wisdom
Then she shows much concern for the nation and our children
She is indeed a godly creation
And we see how hard she strives for greatness.

She sheds light onto all of the darkness
And she does not crave to be acknowledged
Yet we appreciate all of her knowledge
Millions of people admire her courage

And she has been around since the beginning of time.

She is a powerful woman

That walks tall with her head high

She is adorned in confidence

Plus, her skin is enhanced by the sun's magical kiss

This woman is the definition of an Empress

More like your modern day Queen

The most fascinating woman you will ever see...

That is simply because - you've been in the presence of a Queen.

THE CHOSEN ONE

Soft spoken and her words ride like waves stronger than the ocean

Her beauty lights the horizon and you can see the goddess shining from miles away

Yes, I say, she is most definitely chosen.

Chosen because she is most emulated yet she is mistreated and constantly frowned upon

Lied to since day one, however, she still found her way guided by the sun's - rays

I speak for her because she is the chosen one.

Needless to say, her coils are admired like her skin is rich with melanin

The sun strokes the surface to leave it silky bronze and vibrant

Many pretend to be sickened by her complexion

In spite of them flocking to bathe like the lizards

Who do they think that they are fooling?

She is the one,

She is definitely chosen.

It is not camouflaged – it is no secret.

It is not hidden – you can see it.

The cover was removed many moons ago

She is the force that has always given you that inner sight

Love the womb-man

For she is clearly chosen.

THAT GIRL

That girl is spoiled by random men
There is nothing you can tell her
She is living great by their ends
Constant shopping sprees
And her bills are always paid
There is nothing that she wants
So she has no complaints
Spoiled with two cars and house
With a gorgeous vacation home deep in the south

She is that girl
That has the world in her palms
That woman that many envies.
She is that girl indeed.

Many men are mesmerized by her words
They stop and they look in awe
As they are magnetized by her curves
It could be the perfection of her stride
And the attraction of her smile
Possibly the sparkle in her eyes
And the freshness of her style

She is that girl
That has the world in her palms

That woman that many envies.
She is that girl indeed.

She has been the apple of many people's eyes
They say that beauty is her name
Her life seems amazing but it isn't necessarily that way
Inside she cries
Many people judge but do not live her life
She is bitter
She is scorned
She has a sense of loneliness
She is torn
Another beautiful body lost in a cold world

She is that girl
That has the world in her palms
That woman that many envies.
She is that girl indeed.

DEAR BLACK MAN

Dear Black Man,

You are a King

And I am taking the time to tell you

That no matter what goes down

I will always be here for you

Protecting you

Like an Empress is supposed to do

We come from the same struggle

How can I not love you?

You've given me every reason to

From your admirable brown skin

To the kinks in your hair

And the fullness of your lips

There is no being on earth

That can ever compare to you

You are irresistible

And by far you are the most wanted

From the moment you were conceived

You were labeled a public enemy

You became the world's target

A threat to society

For being born strong, Black, and free

But being the public enemy means nothing to me

I will be here as long as you need me to be

I will be here to console you

I will be your shoulder to lean on

Dear Black Man,

I promise you that I mean you no harm

I will continue to speak up for you

And serve in the best interests of you

You will not see or hear of me putting you down

As long as you work hard towards success

I will look on and be proud

Just understand that you have my heart

I will forever love you just the way you are

So please don't ever change unless it's for the better

And don't ever forget that

You and I were put on this earth for each other

I am my brother's keeper.

I love you always my brother...

Proud Of You

I am so proud of my brothers and sisters.

I'm talking about the ones that have done what a lot of people fear.

The ones that chose the entrepreneurship route because their vision is clear.

The ones that choose to be independent...

And do all they can to survive on their own stampeding on fear.

I am proud of you.

I know that times are hard...

Believe me, I know.

I know it seems like no one supports your positive endeavors...

Believe me, I know.

I also know that one day soon all of our brothers and sisters will awaken from their slumber and appreciate your work and dedication.

That time is coming...

One day soon they will spend their dollars with you too.

We will regain our power and become more respected individuals.

Please don't give up on whatever it is that you do.

Understand that this sista right here...

This sista, believes in you.

I am proud of you.

Self-Love

You don't have to love me
Because I love me.
I have gone through so much
And experienced many things.
There is nothing you can say...
There is nothing you can do...
To make me feel anything less
Than powerful.
You will not make me weak...
You will not destroy me...
Or take my self-love away from me.
I am more puissant than you think...
As hard as you try to break me down
I will not fall.
I will not hit rock bottom because I have the greatest love of all.
The love that stems from within...
The love that makes me speak with so much passion...
Coming from my heart and soul...
This kind of love can never be bought or sold.

Alkebulan Love

ALKEBULAN LOVE

I dream of the day that I step off that plane…

I want to see you and breathe you…

Wrap my arms around you…

Your presence reassures me…

Your energy fills me…

The frequency between you and I…

Let's me know that everything is going to be alright…

For years I've been waiting for this day…

As my tears fall, your warm touch will dry them away…

I will lay down on you, close my eyes, and meditate…

Your strength and your vitality…

Your life and our history…

My mind you stimulate…

The love I have will never fade…

Growing stronger by the day…

Many people may not correlate...

Our connection is deeper than your book dates...

Before Common Era...

Before there was a date...

Before there was hate...

Before we were mentally and physically enslaved...

There was you - nothing but you...

Mother Africa, I love you!

WHAT REALLY HAPPENED?

I heard about how caring they are and how they never turned a man down...

I heard about how they openly welcomed foreigners onto their wealthy ground...

I heard about how they take care of all of their people...

I heard about how they once felt like all humans were equal...

I heard about a lot of wars and how every war had a sequel...

I heard about the princes, the princesses, the kings, the queens and the thieves...

I heard about their many accomplishments and the end of their dynasties...

I heard about some strange things, so strange that it made me wonder you see...

I heard about them living in Jungles something like Tarzan and Mowgli...

I heard about them living in huts, with lots of children, in villages filled with love...

So that definitely crosses out the Jungle Story above...

I heard about them reigning supreme for many centuries...

I heard about the many men it took to build those statues you see...

I heard it was so monumental that even the people in Europe could see...

I heard it was so monumental that it attracted the Greeks greed and jealousy...

The Greeks failed to destroy them from the outside, so they did it from within...

They shook the right hands and became the African's friend...

They shook the right hands and became the black man's friend...

Subjugation and then mind control of the people - no shame.

Humiliation of the people and who are they to blame?

For the sudden deaths and plagues...

The rise of Syphilis and AIDS...

Yes, I heard about the women and children being used as sex slaves...

I heard about some people supposedly going to that land to *"fix it"*...

I heard when they left there was, even more, sickness and diseases...

I heard about the natives being hungry, like really starving, and mistreated...

Now please explain to me how did they fix it?

I heard about them being murdered for protecting their sons and daughters…

I heard about them being murdered for not following the pale man's orders…

I heard so many things but yet I still sit back and wonder…

What really happened?

I sit back and I ponder.

MAMA DON'T CRY

When the sun and moon met

You were designed

After years of coming together

You gave us life

And provided us with all the necessities to survive

The lush green land

And clean water at our hands

Beautiful trees across the horizon

We grew with everything that you created

Evolved and then became emulated

In due time it became ourselves that we hated

Assisting in destroying the earth

Carrying on as if we have no worth

They turned their backs on you mama

When you should always be put first

Putting you first means to love our sisters and brothers

Instead they are out there fighting and killing each other

I can feel your pain

Please mama don't cry

Your tears birth oceans that flood my eyes

Each day I pray for unity amongst your children

Soon we will come together in harmony

And bring death to self-destruction.

STRIPPED

The greatest place on earth was created by the Gods

Beautiful is an understatement of how gorgeous you are

There is no other soil like yours

There was no greater air to breathe

With you was the safest place to be

You are blessed with natural resources

And your people had strength like magic

So great it became an attraction

Drawing moonlighters in like magnets

They had no remorse and they took it all

They renamed the countries

Forced people into bondage

They were given new names

And could no longer speak their native language

The madness went on for centuries

In due time things did change

The enslaved finally regained their freedom

Yet their brains still remain in chains

151 years later since freedom has rung

Yet there is still a lot of work to do

Your children are lost

They truly lost their way

Due to the good ole' divide and conquer rule.

Mama Afrika

Your beauty is like no other and you are richer than your thieves

You gave life to the most beautiful beings on earth

You are the Queen.

All hail the Queen

Goddess of life...

You gave me life.

I won't ever turn my back on you as long as my flesh survives

And lives pass the cruelty and hatefulness

No matter what the evilness of this cold world says about you

I know the truth and I know that I have warmth within you.

You are the reason that we are here

And I am so grateful to have come from magnificence like you

You are the air that I choose to breathe

You are the vision that I see...

Mama Afrika, you are the greatest and I will always love you.

The Revolution

SYSTEMATIC GENOCIDE

Goddess of this nation

I'm the bold reflection

Honorable creation

Walk in my direction

Listen to this lesson...

Destroy, Rebuild

Unite as one...

The earth, The moon

The stars

The sun.

Product of the universe,

You're so freaking dangerous.

Melanated, intelligent, full force I'm diligent

360 knowledge, this womb-man is wisdom

Time to lay our laws and create our own system.

The system is poison

Media is corruption

Destroying our people and they're aiming at our children

Young boys in dresses

young girls are groomsmen

They're controlling procreation and our bloodline is ending.

STAND

Stand up for what you believe in

Raise up your fist and start achieving

Say what others won't

Say it loud! They are listening.

If you say it enough they will start believing

They want us to stand up!

But when we stand up they are shooting us down

There is no in between

You're either there because there is no option for here

Or they are shutting shit down!

I am the mother so Claire

I am the Angela no fear

I am the Afeni so dare

Power to the people

We must unite and empower the people

We must unite and destroy all evil

With every war, there is a sequel

I release this positive energy in the free zone

Every day I put it in the air for my people

Stand up if you have a backbone

Make a stand if you're tired of being done wrong

I am the voice if you need one

I am the voice for your freedom

I am the voice just pay attention

Just open your mind and expand some

Make a stand for the revolution.

MIND CONTROL

It's psychological thing,
Imprints and poison to the brain.

Serious mind control,
That is driving the people insane.

We went from praising the Gods,
And having our own brain.

To praising the pale man's God,
Captive bonded with steel chains.

Praising the pale man's God,
Made us forget our true names.

Praising that pale God,
Secured those shackles to your brain.

We went from spirituality,
To being scared of what our ancestors believed.

Giving our children European names,
When they should be more like Hassan and Jikindi.

Leave massa's names for massa's family,
Give your children names like Kumba and Nyambi.

There's nothing greater than being in touch with your roots,
But the system programmed your mind to block out the truth.

The system programmed your mind,
And whitewashed the verisimilitude.

Now you think your black is ugly,
And you don't know what to do.

You think your black is ugly,
So you too whitewash the moving truth.

Your black is beautiful,
But the system has you thinking different.

Your black is beautiful,
So please stop lightening your angelic skin.

Your black is so beautiful
I beg you to continue procreation.

Don't murder that baby.

What they are doing to our warrior class is such a devastation.

They have been humiliating our men,
Forcing on them effeminization.

Causing our women to lose respect,
And that decreases our numbers of propagation.

They kill our men like animals,
And throw them in jail even if they did nothing wrong.

There is a systematic genocide going on.

Wake up

Focus your mind and pay attention.

MELANATED GODDESS

Little with a strong punch
My words speak in volumes
But they don't hear me tho'!

I'm a Melanated Goddess
That was raised in the ghetto
Yet my ancestors were from the black lands
That was once known as Alkebulan
But they don't hear me tho'!

Royalty from the very beginning of time
Yet my people were stripped from time
I'm just here to awake the sleep sheep
The ones that are being feasted on by them beasts

Break those mental chains
Because we together can make a change
You have to want it just as bad as I do

No more talking

We need more action

And it all starts within you!

Deadly Weapon

Read these chapters and tell me about this lesson.

Do this test but don't ask me any questions.

What I say is right and do not dare challenge me like I am wrong.

I am teaching you what I was taught so you need to follow along.

Memorize what you are told

And do what I say and not what you choose to do.

Does any of this sound familiar?

Of course it does...

I know it do...

That is what many hear from their teachers and principals all day long.

Once you get bold enough and start breaking their rules...

You will be punished, looked down upon, and considered a fool...

For exploring outside of the systems indoctrinated rules.

You will be possibly labeled a menace, thug, and a criminal

Suspended, ignored, expelled, or denied...

Credit and loans

Jobs and lucrative careers.

Your resume is strong but they clearly don't care.

You were turned away because of a pale person with naturally straight hair.

Your skin is "too black" and they see those locs in your hair.

For many it's just their hair texture and the light black skin that they wear...

Unapologetically.

Stay proud being yourself

No matter what brown complexion you are... to them you are still a threat.

How are they going to win when you hold so much knowledge?

You're the same "fool" that dropped out of school and later went back to graduate from a historic black college.

And they hate that.

Yes, they fear that kind of knowledge.

They rather you be wild, black, and stupid.

Or a sheep to their laws and regulations.

As long as you're awake and living by your own laws...

The system will view you as a walking deadly weapon.

Stay protected.

Law of Retaliation

Eye for an eye, tooth for a tooth.

That is what many people lived by and they still do.

Eventually on lookers learned to leave well enough alone.

Do not mess with mine and I will not fool with yours.

Many people feel like that is the wrong answer but I say whatever...

Give them what they want!

They keep killing our people so give them what they are asking for...

Violence and more than likely a bloody war...

Is what they are provoking because they know that we are not capable of defeating their army.

There is more of us than there is of them but we still are not ready for that kind of smoke.

Go on strike and stop supporting their businesses.

They are in these positions because we are keeping them rich.

Buy from your own people...

Until our needs and wants are met.

Like justice and we demand ultimate respect.

Peaceful protesting is not doing anything for the lives lost.

We need to hit them where it hurts and never stop.

Their pockets stay swollen because of us...

We're the boss.

They need to stop abusing their power.

Let me be more specific...

I need to be clear.

They need to stop abusing their skin color as well as the uniforms that they wear.

Oppressors come in all shapes, shades, and sizes.

Just because you are black that doesn't mean nothing if you're a part of them.

I see a beautiful melanated person that is so far gone that they have no clue where they come from.

Due to the systematic brainwash you are now a part of the problem and you are no longer the solution.

You joined the law to make a much-needed change...

But you became worse than the original oppressor.

And that's a damn shame.

You are now one of them and retaliation sees no face.

We are emptying pockets and clearing out all safe's.

When the revolution begins our lives will no longer be the same.

We will get back what is ours and plenty more.

As long as we stay on the same accord, we will overcome it all.

About The Poetress

Nikey Pasco-Dunston…

Wife, Mother, Friend, Life Coach, Holistic Healer, Motivational Speaker, Writer, Lyricist and more. The self-proclaimed Empress is here to share her adoration of writing with you. A woman who wears many hats well and has a passion for naturally healing wounds. The Empress grew a love for writing stories in Kindergarten and picked up her love for poetry in her 2nd Grade year. In 1993, Youth Pathways awarded her the "Short Story Award" and she has written countless unpublished stories and poems since then.

If you are interested in getting a daily dose of Queenism or to simply learn more about the Empress visit her website and follow her on Facebook, Twitter, & Instagram.

www.nikeypasco.com

www.facebook.com/onlynikeypasco

Twitter: @NikeyPasco

Instagram: @NikeyPasco

"Usually you have to go through a severe storm for you to truly appreciate the sun."

-Nikey Pasco-Dunston

Also by Nikey Pasco-Dunston

An urban non-fiction story that is intertwined with self-help to assist in bringing out the best in you.

AVAILABLE NOW ON AMAZON & AMAZON KINDLE!

Now What Are Your Thoughts?

Which poem is your favorite and why?

_____

_____

Which poem is your least favorite and why?

_____

_____

What do you want to see me write more about
in my next poetic collection?

_____

_____

Please tweet me your thoughts and use the
hash tag #WOMW

61668627R00057

Made in the USA
Charleston, SC
26 September 2016